THE COMPLETE HANDBOOK
for Planning, Implementing and Sustaining

Frank MacGrath

THE COMPLETE HANDBOOK *for Planning, Implementing and Sustaining a Successful Fundraising Golf Tournament*
Copyright © 2007 Civil Sector Press and Frank MacGrath

All rights reserved. No part of this publication may be reproduced, stored in any material form (including photocopying or storing it in any medium by electronic means and whether or not transiently or incidentally to some other use of this publication) without the written permission of the copyright holder except in accordance with the provisions of the Copyright Act. Applications for the copyright holder's written permission to reproduce any part of this publication should be addressed to the publisher.

Warning: The doing of an unauthorized act in relation to a copyrighted work may result in both a civil claim for damages and criminal prosecution.

Important:

The following materials are intended as general reference tools for understanding the underlying principles of gift planning. The opinions expressed herein are solely those of the authors. To ensure the currency of the information presented, readers are strongly encouraged to solicit the assistance of appropriate professionals.

Further, any examples or sample forms presented are intended only as illustrations. The authors, publisher and their agents assume no responsibility for errors or omissions or for damages arising from the use of published information or opinions.

ISBN 1-895589-51-7

Published by Civil Sector Press
Box 86, Station C,
Toronto, Ontario, M6J 3M7 Canada
Telephone: 416-345-9403
Fax: 416-345-8010

Printed in Canada by:
Design by: Creative by Nature

THE COMPLETE HANDBOOK
for Planning, Implementing and Sustaining

A Successful FUNDRAISING GOLF TOURNAMENT

Frank MacGrath

Copyright © 2007 Civil Sector Press and Frank MacGrath

All rights reserved. No part of this publication may be reproduced or transmitted in any form or by any means, electronic or mechanical, including photocopy, recording or any information storage and retrieval system now known or to be invented, without the prior written permission of the publisher and author, except by a reviewer who wishes to quote brief passages in connection with a review written for inclusion in a magazine, newspaper, or broadcast, and any such reproduction or transmission without the prior written permission of the publisher and author is a violation of copyright law.

Any request for such reproduction or transmission of any portion or portions of this book should be directed in writing to the publisher: Civil Sector Press, Box 86, Station C, Toronto, Ontario Canada M6J 3M7.

ISBN 1-895589-51-7

Author: Frank MacGrath
Cover and page design: Creative by Nature

Table of Contents

SECTION	CHAPTER	PAGE
	Introduction	1
A	Getting Started – Setting Objectives for your Tournament	7
B	Building and Maintaining a Great Organizing Committee	13
C	Creating a Realistic Planning Timeline	21
D	Choosing The Right Golf Course	29
E	Making Money – Setting Your Tournament Budget	37
F	Determining Your Tournament Format – What, When & How	47
G	Alternative Formats For Golf Fundraising Events	57
H	On-Course Activities – Keep it Fun & Keep it Simple	63
I	Hole-In-One Contests	71
J	Marketing & Branding Your Tournament	79
K	Sponsorship Support – The Key to a Profitable Event	91
L	Golfer Gifts & Prizes	101
M	Fundraising Activities at the Tournament	111
N	Immediately Prior to the Tournament	121
O	Volunteer Management	129

SECTION	CHAPTER	PAGE
P	ON THE FIRST TEE - DAY-OF-EVENT MANAGEMENT	137
Q	BIRDIES & BOGEYS - CONTINGENCY PLANNING/PITFALLS TO AVOID	147
R	THE SCORECARD - TOURNAMENT REVIEW AND FOLLOW UP	155
S	GOOD TO GREAT – TAKING YOIR TOURNAMENT TO THE NEXT LEVEL	161
T	HOW GTI CAN FURTHER ASSIST YOUR ORGANIZATION	169

Introduction

Introduction

Over the past twenty years, the growth of charity golf tournaments across North America has been phenomenal. The Golf Tournament Association of America estimates that there are more than 1 million "golf outings" in the United States each year. In Canada, despite a relatively shorter golf season, most 18-hole public courses host at least 100 or more golf tournaments each year, the majority of which are charity golf tournaments that raise substantial funds for a wide variety of non-profit organizations. While these golf tournaments can offer tremendous fundraising and awareness-building opportunities for many non-profit organizations, they are also large-scale "special events" that require a great deal of staff resources, volunteer manpower and financial commitment.

The purpose of this handbook is to assist you and your colleagues in planning, executing and maintaining a very successful charity golf tournament. Having coordinated more than 400 successful golf tournaments in the past ten years, Golf Tournaments Inc. has prepared this handbook in order to assist volunteers and professional fundraising staff within nonprofit organizations who are new to the experience of organizing a charity golf tournament. This updated 2007 version of the handbook will also be beneficial to those staff members or volunteers who are already familiar with organizing their own golf event but who want to take their tournament "to the next level".

A CIVIL SECTOR PRESS HANDBOOK

In the following pages, this handbook will outline the specific components of tournament planning, coordination and implementation that you and your fellow volunteers and staff colleagues should consider when putting together your tournament, whether it is a first time event or whether you are looking to take your tournament from "good to great".

See you on the first tee!

Frank MacGrath

President & CEO
Golf Tournaments Incorporated

SECTION A

Getting Started – Setting Objectives for your Tournament

SECTION A

Getting Started – Setting Objectives for your Tournament

So you want to host a charity golf tournament for your organization? Before you get buried in the minutiae of tournament details such as selecting a golf course, preparing marketing materials and securing sponsors, it is important that your organization analyze the reasons that have motivated you to hold a golf tournament. As you begin the process of planning your golf tournament, we suggest that you consider the following questions:

- What is the main objective(s) of this tournament – is it to raise funds for your organization? To build awareness of your organization? Both? Are there any other reasons?

- What is the financial goal of the tournament in terms of net profit? While this may be difficult to specify, particularly for a brand new event, it is important to carefully consider whether a charity golf tournament is the most appropriate kind of special event by which your organization will raise funds.

- What kind of tournament will best achieve these goals? We suggest you look at the traditional 18 hole, 144 golfer "shotgun start" format as well as considering other options (e.g. 9 hole mini tournament).

- How can you differentiate your event from the large number of charitable golf tournaments held each year? What specific factors (e.g. choice of golf course, price, event format, etc.) will entice golfers and sponsors to choose to support your charity tournament and to return each year?

- What resources (volunteers, staff, knowledge of golf, contacts) does your organization have available to meet these objectives?

- Certain tournaments "plateau" after a number of successful years. How can your organization keep your tournament "new and exciting" each year?

Setting out specific objectives will help all volunteers and staff involved in this tournament understand what your organization is trying to achieve and will allow you and your organization to measure the results after the tournament is completed. For existing tournaments, we recommend that the organization review its tournament objectives each year to ensure that these objectives are still current with the needs of the organization.

SECTION B

Building and Maintaining a Great Organizing Committee

SECTION B
Building and Maintaining a Great Organizing Committee

For new tournaments, it is strongly recommended that an "Organizing Committee" be formed to carry out the coordination and implementation of all aspects of the golf tournament. The following issues should be considered in creating this Committee:

a) **Size** - a 4-6 person Committee is ideal, allowing for delegation of duties amongst a variety of Committee members so that no single volunteer is unduly burdened. The committee can be comprised of volunteers, staff members and/or other supporters of your organization.

b) **Chairperson:** the Committee should appoint a chairperson to lead the meetings and chair these sessions. The Committee may also want to appoint one or more vice-chairs to assist the chair.

c) **Staff Support:** a staff liaison or support person should be appointed to work with the committee, so that there is ongoing communication between this new group and the organization that will benefit from the tournament. If a staff member within your organization is taking the lead role in the tournament coordination, it is crucial for that person to communicate with the committee which key tasks he/she will be focusing on and which key tasks the committee members need to focus on.

d) **Role of the Committee**: the Committee should oversee all aspects of the tournament's organization, but its main efforts should focus primarily on the following areas:

- Initial course selection and tournament pricing
- tournament format and itinerary
- securing sponsors
- obtaining prizes
- recruiting golfers
- fundraising activities at the tournament (e.g. raffle/auction, day-of-event sales)
- unique ideas to enhance the tournament
- event review

To effectively manage these key areas, the committee can choose "chairs" or "leads" to be responsible for each area (e.g. Prize Chairman). The following tasks should each be delegated to one committee member:

- liaison with the golf course
- menu selection
- marketing/advertising (media announcements, website & email blasts)
- contingency planning
- day-of-event management & volunteers

It is helpful if the Committee contains at least a few members who are knowledgeable golfers who have played in other charity golf tournaments; however, it is not necessary that every Committee member be an avid or accomplished golfer.

For the more established tournament, the particular duties of the committee should be reevaluated each year to focus on the key priorities that committee is facing (e.g. drop off in sponsorship, attracting more golfers).

d) **Meetings:** the Committee should begin meeting at least 4-6 months in advance of the tournament date and meet thereafter on a regular basis as decided by the Committee. The most effective Committees communicate between meetings to follow up on the tasks outlined at the previous meeting and to ensure that the organizational timeline is being followed.

e) **Recruiting Your Committee:** to recruit the organizing committee look to your Board of Directors (current and former), volunteer base and friends of the organization. Ask some golfers you know to get involved, including suppliers and partners that work with your organization.

Maintaining a Strong Organizing Committee

One of the most difficult tasks any annual golf tournament faces is maintaining a strong and interested golf committee, and keeping these volunteers motivated year after year. Some suggestions to keep your key volunteers actively participating on the golf committee are:

- Tangibly thank them – a post tournament round of golf might be a great way to wrap up your event, in addition to recognizing them at the tournament;

- Ask each committee member if he/she will support the tournament again by serving on the committee and get their input as to what specific areas they would like to focus on;

- Rotate positions so the committee members take on different tasks and develop different skill sets;

- Create a succession plan – ask a retiring committee member to help find their successor.

- Cultivate a champion within the committee – ideally this is a key volunteer who helps you keep the tournament focused on getting better and better (and more profitable) each year.

 *Pro's Tip*

✓ *Keep the meetings focused (use an agenda), brief (set a time limit), and fun.*

✓ *Appoint a committee member to summarize in a brief one-page memo following each meeting, what decisions were made and what actions were to be implemented & by whom. Then Circulate these minutes to all committee members by email.*

✓ *If "in person" meetings are logistically difficult, consider using conference calls.*

SECTION C
CREATING A REALISTIC PLANNING TIMELINE

SECTION C

Creating a Realistic Planning Timeline

An overall event timeline should be established so that everyone involved knows which tasks have to be completed, by whom and when. The following timeline is a sample schedule for a brand new tournament.

6 Months in Advance	• Follow up phone calls to Committee re: all tasks outstanding
	• Review all areas of delegated tasks - progress reports
	• Focus on tasks not yet completed
5 Months	• 2nd Committee meeting
	• Finalize promotional materials
	• Confirm player registration fee and sponsorship levels
	• First solicitation letter to sponsors and prize donors
	• First mailing/emailing to potential golfers
	• Confirm involvement of celebrities or media participants

4 Months	• Measure progress to date on sponsors/prizes/golfers • Prepare 2nd mailing/email blast • Get your committee members following up with their leads by phone and email
3 Months	• 3rd Committee meeting • Second mailing/email blast goes out • Site tour at selected golf course • Press releases distributed • Measure the success to date (golfer registrations and confirmed sponsors) versus the event budget expectations
2 Months	• 4th Committee meeting • Start to pick up prizes/auction items • Email the tournament itinerary to all registered participants • Final meeting with golf course staff • (Reference Section N for a more detailed task list of all items to be covered off in the final 30 days)

1 Month	• 5th Committee meeting
	• Finalize all logistical arrangements
	• Email the tournament itinerary to all registered participants
	• (Reference Section N for a more detailed task list of all items to be covered off in the final 30 days)
2 weeks Prior to Event	• Final Committee meeting prior to the tournament
	• Finalize day-of-event preparations
	• Design and produce all printed materials for the tournament (e.g. signage, program, rule sheet, etc)
	• Finalize names of all golfers participating
	• Final site meeting at the golf course

Post-Event	• Complete collection of any outstanding monies
	• Review meeting with Committee and thank your volunteers
	• Review meeting with the golf course
	• Secure the course/date for next year's event
	• Update your website to thank sponsors & golfers and post pictures
	• Send out thank you letters and tax receipts (as applicable)*
	• Begin preparations for next year's tournament

For existing tournaments, the timeline can be condensed but it is still very important to secure your course and date relatively quickly after the conclusion of the previous tournament. In addition, it is advantageous to your organization to let your sponsors, golfers and prize donors know the date of your next golf event early so it can be incorporated into everyone's calendar and budget planning cycle.

* *Please refer to Canada Revenue Agency Guidelines to ensure you are complying appropriately.*

SECTION D

Choosing the Right Golf Course

SECTION D

Choosing the Right Golf Course

One of the most important decisions in planning a charity golf tournament is the selection of the golf course at which the event will be held. The following is a checklist of criteria and helpful hints to be used in this research and selection process:

Getting Started

- Start early: most golf courses offer a right of first refusal to returning tournaments, so if your event is a new tournament you should approach courses in which you are interested in September/October/November of the year preceding your tournament.

- Ask committee members, friends and colleagues for suggestions about "good tournament courses" in your local area.

- Consider the type of course at which you wish to hold your event – public, semi-private or private.

- Many private courses allow tournaments only on a restricted basis (e.g. only one day per week) and some private courses do not allow any tournaments at all. Also, private courses will often require the endorsement of one of their club members to bring your tournament request to the Club's Board of Directors or Golf Committee for approval. Public courses usually have a designated 'tournament coordinator' with whom your organization can deal directly.

Course Research

- Once you have determined a list of courses to approach, call and obtain their tournament price package.

- Most courses will offer combined pricing for green fees/carts and some include meals directly in the tournament package. Some courses may only allow tournaments at certain times of year and/or if a meal of a certain value is included.

- Prices will vary significantly, depending on the caliber of the golf course and on site facilities. Like hotels, there is a wide range of options from low end to moderate to high end.

- A key criteria in the course selection will be the size of the tournament and the starting method; ask each prospective course for their various options for different size groups of golfers.

- Compare the various courses based on location, accessibility, price, date availability, reputation, etc.

- The Internet is a very useful source of information about golf course pricing, location, amenities, etc. Most golf courses have their own website which will include a lot of detailed information about their tournament packages, on site facilities and location.

Course Visits/Site Inspection

- Once the list of potential courses is reduced to a short list of 3-4 courses, 2-3 Committee members should visit these courses and determine the following:

- Key contact personnel for golf/catering matters - is it the golf pro? Banquet manager? Both?

- Does the course have a specific "tournament coordinator?"

- Is the clubhouse a sufficient size for reception/meal purposes?

- On site facilities - driving range? practice green?

- Location - how accessible is the course? Proximity to hotel if required?

- Is the course planning any renovations to either the golf course or the clubhouse before, during or after your tournament date;

- Availability of each course for your preferred tournament dates?

- Is there any other event or tournament taking place at the course that day?

- You may also want to ask these courses for 2-3 references from other similar charitable organizations who have held charity golf events at this facility.

Contract Negotiation

Once you have selected a course, you will need to enter into a written contract with the golf course. In executing this contract please note the following:

- Ask for the contract in writing, including payment schedule.

- What deposit amount is required and when is the balance due? (many courses will require payment in full prior to the event)

- What taxes/gratuities are charged on golf, carts, meals, liquor/beer, beverages? (This may vary from province to province)
- Are there any mandatory purchase requirements from the pro shop?
- When are confirmed numbers required for golfers? Meals?

Golf Course Liaison

After the course is selected and a contract confirmed, assign one Committee member to be the chief liaison to the golf course. As the tournament date approaches this Committee member should update the golf course on the progress of the event including:

- number of golfers attending
- any specific sponsor requests (e.g. Coke product to be sold instead of Pepsi as Coke is a major sponsor of your tournament)
- special on-course contests
- special dietary requirements

Pro's Tips

✓ *Keep in mind that the golf course staff are generally experienced in dealing with tournament groups and can be a great source of assistance and advice. However, as they are dealing with multiple events, it is important to put all requests in writing and to keep the golf course staff apprised of any special requirements (e.g. audio-visual equipment) that you need fulfilled.*

✓ *Most host courses will provide prizes for your tournament in support of the business revenue you are providing to that course. Ask the course well in advance what "prize support" they can provide to you.*

✓ *Many courses offer reduced green fee rates at the beginning and end of their seasons. Ask the course if this is an option for your tournament.*

✓ *Familiarization rounds – most courses will offer your organization a complimentary "familiarization round" if you are not familiar with their course. Use this round to bring out some committee members and test drive the golf course.*

SECTION E

Making Money – Setting Your Tournament Budget

SECTION E

Making Money – Setting Your Tournament Budget

Setting a detailed tournament budget will help your organization to properly assess the projected revenues, expenses and net profit to be derived from this event. Enclosed is a very basic sample draft budget. The tournament budget should include the following details:

Revenues

a) **Player Registration Fee:** your organization needs to determine what "registration fee" is marketable in your geographic area, while still covering all "hard costs" (green fees, power carts, meals, taxes, etc) and providing a per player financial contribution over and above that cost, so that each registration contributes to your overall net profit. While registration fees for charity tournaments will vary from city to city and course to course, it is important to bear in mind the "market rate" of a round of golf, cart, lunch and dinner at the chosen course. Many tournaments then add a range of $25-$50 over and above those costs as the basis for the tournament registration fee. The Committee might want to research what other charity golf tournaments have charged at the selected course in determining the player registration fee. You should also get a sense from your committee members what the golfers likely to be invited to this tournament will be willing to pay to participate. This will help not only with budget planning, but also with selecting a golf course that meets your group's pricing expectations.

b) **Sponsorship Revenue:** Section K deals with sponsorship in more detail. However, for budget purposes we recommend that sponsors be divided into categories and that any benefits given to sponsors (e.g. complimentary foursome for a title sponsor) be recognized in the budget either as "less player registration revenue" or "additional player costs".

c) **Day-of-Event Fundraising & On-Course Activities:** In Section M several specific on-course activities are outlined which can raise money the day of the tournament. These activities include sales of contest packages at registration, mulligans, raffle and draw tickets.

d) **Auction:** many tournaments will have either a silent or live auction (and some events have both). The Committee should assign two members to coordinate what items will be auctioned and if it will be done via a silent bid (signing up on a sheet) or via live bid run by the emcee or auctioneer. See Section M for more details on Auctions at golf tournaments.

e) **Donations:** Some corporations or individuals who wish to support your organization either may not golf or may not be able to attend on your tournament date. Ensure that your registration package includes the option for a direct "DONATION".

Expenses

There are a number of specific expense categories that your budget should include:

a) **Tournament Packages/Shotgun Fees:** most courses will provide a set rate for green fees/power carts/driving range/taxes. As discussed in Section D re: Golf Course Selection, obtain a written estimate from the golf course showing the breakdown in costs and related taxes between these various items.

b) **Meals:** your budget should include taxes and gratuities on all meals as well as any extra meals for non-golfers/volunteers. Your budget should include a provision if any beverages (e.g. wine with dinner) are being provided.

c) **Pro Shop Credit Charges:** some courses require a mandatory prize purchase (e.g. $5.00/golfer) from the pro shop. If this is the case, then this cost is a tournament expense.

d) **Sponsor Signage:** there will be costs associated with sponsor hole signage, banners, recognition plaques to sponsors, etc. This can be $1000 or more, depending on the quantity and quality of signage required. Your organization may want to consider obtaining an "in kind" sponsor (e.g. local printer) who will donate the required signage in return for sponsor recognition at the event.

e) **Golfer Gift:** if your organization plans to purchase a gift for each golfer (e.g. golf shirt at registration) this expense should be factored into the budget.

f) Prize Contingency: although your objective is to have all prizes donated, your budget should carry a small contingency allowance in case it is necessary to purchase any last minute prizes to complete your prize table.

g) Administrative costs for printing, mailing, event supplies, etc.

h) Miscellaneous: it is a good idea to carry a contingency of between 2.5 – 5% of the expense total for any unforeseen expenses, especially for a new tournament.

 Pro's Tip

✓ *When setting your tournament registration fees, ask the host golf course what other charity tournaments are charging their golfers for their tournaments at that course.*

✓ *Make sure you are aware of the golf course's payment schedule so the cash flow from the tournament revenue meets the timing of expenses incurred from this event.*

✓ *Taxation will vary from province to province and state to state. Check with your organization's Chief Financial Officer or Treasurer as to what taxes need to be applied on which items, and whether any of those taxes can be recovered by your organization.*

✓ *Tax receipts - can the recipient charity provide income tax receipts to participating sponsors and/or golfers? Tax legislation and regulation varies greatly from jurisdiction to jurisdiction, so ensure that you research this carefully in advance of your event.*

Please check with Canada Revenue Agency to determine what is applicable to your situation.

SECTION F
Determining Your Tournament Format – What, When & How

SECTION F

Determining Your Tournament Format – What, When & How

There are a wide variety of golf tournament formats that can be used at a charity golf tournament. In its initial meetings the Committee should focus on the issues of tournament format and itinerary and decide on the following:

- In what month will the tournament be held?

- Will the tournament be a weekday or weekend event?

- Will the tournament be the more traditional "afternoon of golf followed by dinner" or a morning of golf followed by lunch?

- Is the tournament to be "individual stroke play" where every golfer plays his/her own ball, or will it be a team competition (foursome plays together in a scramble format).

- Does the golf course you've chosen allow each tournament to choose its format, or is one specific format required?

- Can you give your golfers the option of choosing their own format, and if so, how does this impact upon the golf prizes to be awarded?

Picking the "Right" Date

There is no "best" month in which to hold your tournament. Rather, the decision on when to hold your event will likely be more influenced by your organization's own calendar of events, your local climate and availability at the selected course. However, in choosing the timing for your tournament, we would recommend that you consider factors such as religious holidays, school holidays and competition from other major charity tournaments that may adversely impact attendance at your tournament.

Most corporate/charity tournaments are held on a weekday and most often on a Tuesday, Wednesday or Thursday. Many courses offer a reduced rate on Mondays, but Monday can also be a harder day to "sell" to the corporate community. Many courses also use Monday as a primary day for on-course maintenance. Fridays are also a viable option, although it is often harder to keep as many golfers around for a Friday evening dinner. Many courses also charge a premium for tournaments held on a Friday, Saturday or Sunday. Course availability will vary as certain courses allow tournaments only on certain days while other golf clubs allow tournaments throughout the week. Private courses that allow tournaments generally will not permit them on weekends.

Shotgun Start versus Tee Times

A shotgun start format is usually employed for a golf tournament of 120-144 golfers on 18 holes. Each foursome is assigned a starting hole and begins the tournament at that hole. For example group 5A is the first group on the fifth hole. They would play holes 5-18 consecutively, then play holes 1-4 and this cover all 18 holes. The "5B" foursome would follow them in the same order. In this shotgun start format, the course sounds a "horn" or "gun" to signify the start of play.

For smaller tournaments (e.g. 40-80 golfers) the golf course will likely assign tee times or use a double tee (groups start on either the 1st or 10th tee, but still play all 18 holes). It is very important to discuss these various options with the golf course when planning your event. Similarly, your organization will need to decide whether or not you wish to hold a morning or afternoon tournament.

Sample Tournament Day Itinerary for Shotgun Tournament

A morning event will usually proceed as follows:

7:00 AM	Registration Opens
	Warm up on Driving Range
7:30 AM	Shotgun start (allow 5.5 hours to complete the round)
1:00 PM	Reception
1:30 PM	Lunch
2:00 PM	Prize Table/Auction/Remarks
2:30 PM	Conclusion

An afternoon event will usually proceed as follows:

10:30 AM	Registration Opens/Warm up on Driving Range
12:00 Noon	BBQ Lunch
1:00 PM	PM Shotgun Start (allow 5.5 hours to complete round)
6:30 PM	PM Reception
7:15 PM	PM Dinner
8:00 PM	PM Prize Table/Auction/Remarks
9:00 PM	PM Conclusion

 *Pro's Tip*

✓ Confirm the exact starting times with the course as this may vary depending on the course's requirements.

✓ Most golfers want to warm up when they get to the course so include use of the driving range in the tournament package. Discuss with the course if a section of the range needs to be set aside for your tournament golfers as there may be lessons or other golfers on the range at that time.

- ✓ Having lunch prior to the afternoon golf event helps ensure everyone is there on time.

- ✓ Don't go too late into the evening as people are tired after a long day at the course and likely have to work the next morning. A guideline to use for a 144-person shotgun is that your event should be completely finished (dinner, prizes, auction, remarks) approximately 8 hours after the start of the shotgun (e.g. a 1 pm shotgun event should end by 9 pm)

- ✓ Keep Your Schedule Tight & Focused - no golfer has ever complained that "the tournament ended too early!"

Tournament Format

Check with the golf course to see if there are any restrictions on the type of format that can be used as some courses only allow certain types of formats. If you are unsure about the ability of your group of golfers, assume that there will be a wide range of experience and competency levels. A scramble format is probably the best option, particularly in a larger tournament, as it allows golfers of all abilities to play together. A scramble works as follows:

Each foursome plays as a team. Each golfer tees off and the foursome then selects the best drive. All players in the group play the 2nd shot from the spot of the best drive, and this process is repeated until the ball is holed out. The team then records one team score for each hole. It is a good idea to require a minimum number of drives to be contributed by each golfer per foursome as this involves everyone and mitigates a great golfer from dominating his team's score.

There are a variety of scramble versions which can be applied; it is important to discuss the format you want with the club pro well in advance of your event.

Some tournaments prefer to use an individual stroke play format where each golfer is "playing their own ball." There are various easy-to-use handicapping scoring systems that can be provided by the golf course professional staff to determine low gross and low net winners.

 Pro's Tip

- ✓ *Whatever format is chosen should be clearly spelled out on the "welcome sheet" that is given to each golfer at the tournament. This is the best way to communicate the tournament rules to all golfers and ensure scoring is done fairly and accurately.*

- ✓ *Make sure that the golf course professional staff are fully aware of your tournament format and your expectations for the pace of play.*

- ✓ If your tournament utilizes individual stroke play, do not request or rely on individual golfer's handicaps as most participants will not have a certified handicap for their golf score.

- ✓ The tournament format should be clearly outlined in all tournament marketing materials.

SECTION G

Alternative Formats For Golf Fundraising Events

SECTION G

Alternative Formats For Golf Fundraising Events

This handbook is focused primarily on the more traditional "18-hole" charity golf tournament. However, there are several other options that your organization may want to consider if it does not want to pursue an 18 hole event but does want to raise money through a golf activity. The following is a very brief overview of alternative forms of "golf fundraising":

- Hole-In-One Contest at a local driving range (see section I for details on how Hole-In-One contests work)

- Nine-Hole Tournament – very similar to the 18-hole event but it covers only 9 holes and is therefore less costly.

- Indoor Golf/Mini Putt Contest – a great winter activity at a local indoor mini putt facility. Sell tickets and allow "golfers" to come out and putt in support of your charity.

- Golf Marathons – these usually involve a smaller group of 25-30 golfers trying to play 100 holes each in one day. Funds are raised by having each golfer raise a minimum amount of pledges (similar to a charity walkathon or run).

For the more competitive golf event, you can create a 2/3/4 day tournament modeled after a PGA event. This will require substantially more financial investment and staff/volunteer resources, but it can also reap tremendous benefits for your organization.

SECTION H
ON-COURSE ACTIVITIES – KEEP IT FUN & KEEP IT SIMPLE

SECTION H

On-Course Activities – Keep it Fun & Keep it Simple

During the actual tournament itself there are a number of on-course activities that can take place to enhance your event. In determining these activities, the Committee should consider the following:

- How many activities should there be on-course?

- How will these activities impact the pace of play?

- What resources (e.g. volunteers, equipment) will be required to properly execute these activities?

- Are any or all of these activities included in the registration fee, or is there an additional cost for certain events?

- How will these activities enhance the value of the "golfer's experience" that day?

- How can these activities create greater awareness of, or interest in, your particular organization?

Sample Types Of On-Course Activities

There are two main types of on-course activities at most charity golf tournaments:

- **Traditional Golf Skill Contests** - such as Longest Drive, Closest to the Pin, Hole-In-One, Putting Contest, Beat the Pro, etc. Variations of these contests include "Straightest Drive", "Closest to the Line", Chipping Contest, etc.

- **Customized or Unique Hole Activities** - these are more creative "fun" activities that can take place at a specific hole. Examples include: Par 3 Gambling Hole (golfer bets to land his/her tee shot on the green), Closest to the (prize item located in the fairway).

In addition, some organizations will also incorporate a specific on-course activity to promote awareness about their organization (e.g. a local hospital setting up a blood pressure checkpoint on one hole, a trivia contest featuring trivia questions about the charity).

The golfers attending your event recognize that it is a charity fundraising tournament and that part of the overall objective of the tournament is to raise as much money as possible. The Committee should carefully consider what activities it wants to include and whether there will be an additional cost for these activities to each golfer. Three options to consider are:

- Make the registration fee all-inclusive - a golfer pays one fee in advance and is not asked for money "on the course." This does not include the post-golf raffle and/or auction.

- Sell an "all inclusive" golf contest package to each golfer as they register. For example, a $20 ticket might include 2 mulligans, Hole-In-One Contest, Beat the Pro, water insurance, etc.

- Charge for some or all of the contests individually.

Less is More

A common mistake that many tournament organizers make is to try and do too much out on the golf course. One of the most common complaints about charity golf tournaments from the participants is that the events take too long, and certain on-course activities can add to the backlog on the course. In determining what kind of on-course activities you will have, we recommend that you carefully consider the following factors:

- number of golfers in your event and their level of ability

- keep the on-course activities simple and easy to understand as this will save time on-course and help maintain a quick pace of play;

- discuss your proposed on-course activities in detail with the golf course and get their input as to where such activities should take place on the course, what equipment/set is needed and how it will be staffed or managed;

 *Pro's Tip*

✓ You may want to have Men's and Women's categories for certain on-course contests, especially Longest Drive, where the men and women are teeing off from different locations.

✓ Tell your golfers which activities are at which holes both on the "rule sheet" on each cart and by specific signage at those holes where possible.

- ✓ Most golf courses are now "licensed" to sell beer and liquor products on-course via roving beverage cart. Whether or not your group wants this cart to be available to your golfers (and if so, whether it is a host bar/cash bar) should be discussed with the golf course. Similarly, the committee should review if alcohol at the event is to be provided to golfers free of charge or on a "cash bar" basis.

- ✓ You may want to take photographs of each foursome. Discuss with a few photographers the options and costs for foursome photos, digital photos, etc. These photos can easily be converted into a powerpoint presentation at the tournament dinner and/or uploaded to your organization's website following the event.

- ✓ Similarly, videotaping the tournament for playback at the post-golf reception is quite popular. There are many commercial digital/video and photography services available that offer such products.

SECTION I
HOLE-IN-ONE CONTESTS

SECTION I
Hole-In-One Contests

The "Hole-In-One" contest is a traditional staple at many golf events. While the potential of a Hole-In-One prize offers a great opportunity for your golfers, there is also substantial financial risk to your organization from this particular type of activity if the contest is not carefully planned and properly executed.

Organizing a Hole-In-One Contest

Hole-In-One prizes are primarily based on insurance coverage. For example, at the ABC Charity Golf Classic, the local bank is offering a $10,000 cash prize for a Hole-In-One in the tournament. The bank (or the tournament) will have purchased an insurance policy to pay the $10,000 to the lucky winner. However, most standard insurance policies for Hole-In-One contests require the following:

- a copy of the scorecard from the golf course confirming the length of the hole. It is usually at least 150 yards in length and many policies now require 175 yards. Please check this requirement carefully.

- If the insurance is being arranged through a third party sponsor (e.g. the bank in this example), ask for a copy of the Hole-In-One insurance coverage.

- Confirm who is paying for the insurance.

- Most policies require at least one non-golfing volunteer to be stationed at the tee to serve as the Official Witness and watch each shot. In most instances, this volunteer will need to be at least 18 years old. Some policies require a witness at both the tee and the green so please read the fine print carefully.

- The Hole-In-One prize will only be awarded to the FIRST golfer in the tournament recording a legitimate Hole-In-One. The insurance coverage usually specifies this restriction.

- Professional golfers are generally not allowed to compete in contests.

- Each golfer only gets one attempt at the Hole-In-One. If they take a Mulligan or second shot from the tee at this hole, it would not count for the purposes of the contest.

- To protect your organization and yourself, we recommend that the rule sheet given to each golfer clearly state the rules of the Hole-In-One contest. These rules should be announced by the witness at the tee as each foursome comes through the contest.

- Some tournaments will offer more than one Hole-In-One contest (e.g. a Hole-In-One opportunity at each par 3). Be sure to carefully obtain and review the insurance requirements for all of these different contests as each individual Hole-In-One contest will require the conditions noted above to be met.

19th Hole Shootouts

Some tournaments will offer a "19th" hole shootout immediately following the round of golf, wherein a small number of selected golfers may have qualified to take a chance to compete shot-for-shot for a very large prize (e.g. $1 million dollars). Again we recommend that you very carefully review the insurance requirements associated with such a contest. In addition to the conditions noted above, with a significantly larger prize there will likely be additional requirements such as having an accredited golf pro as a witness, as well as having the entire contest videotaped.

 *Pro's Tip*

- ✓ *With regard to the Hole-In-One coverage and insurance provisions, ask for all details in writing so that there are no surprises.*

- ✓ *Be extra cautious in instructing your witnesses as to their responsibilities.*

- ✓ *Cars and vehicles are popular Hole-In-One prizes. Be sure to confirm with the car dealer sponsoring the Hole-In-One contest whether the prize is a lease of the car or an outright win of that vehicle.*

SECTION J
Marketing & Branding Your Tournament

SECTION J

Marketing & Branding Your Tournament

Think of your golf tournament as a huge marketing and branding opportunity for your organization. You can use the pre-event marketing, day of the tournament and post-event follow up as distinct opportunities through which you can build tremendous awareness of your organization.

Pre-Tournament Marketing

There are several ways to effectively market the tournament, especially in its first year of existence so that you attract the greatest number of golfers, prize donors and sponsors that the tournament can accommodate.

Create a Tournament Invitation/Brochure

A key element of a successful tournament is the invitation package sent to prospective golfers and sponsors. This marketing material should convey enough information about the tournament to answer a potential participant's questions on the following issues:

- tournament date and location
- price/entry fee
- what does the golfer receive for that price?

- details on the designated charity - where are the proceeds going? (be as specific as possible).

- tournament format and itinerary (e.g. 1:00 PM Shotgun Start)

- details on sponsorship opportunities

- contact numbers - phone/fax/email if more information is required

- information on the tournament website and/or online registration options

In addition, a cover letter should be included, asking the recipient for their support, and outlining the various ways in which they can support the tournament. Make the invitation package available in both hard copy and electronic format (e.g. PDF file) so you can distribute the invitations as widely as possible.

Marketing the Tournament

The following is a list of ways through which the tournament can be promoted by individual Committee members and your organization:

- Network via the Committee - have each member send out personal letters to their own network of contacts;

- Mail to your organization's existing database of donors, friends & supporters

- Enlist support from community newspapers, cable TV, and radio public service announcements that will promote the tournament and your organization
- Issue a press release to announce the event (Is a celebrity involved? Where is the money going?)
- Focus on selling in foursomes (144 golfers sounds like a lot, but it is really only 36 teams)
- Source a celebrity endorsement - is there a well-known local athlete/entertainer/media personality who would lend their name to this event?
- Create a specific website for the tournament and indicate the website address in all tournament marketing
- Offer online registration through the tournament website or your organization's website
- Send out regular email blasts and evites
- Ensure that the printed materials can also be emailed to the networks described above and easily downloaded by prospective golfers, donors & sponsors
- Ask local service clubs (Rotary, Kiwanis, Lions) and business clubs to promote the event to their members

Measure the Marketing

In order to measure what forms of marketing were most effective, ask golfers as they register, "How did you hear about this event?" "What made you want to participate?" "Did you visit our golf website?"

Marketing Your Organization at the Tournament

The day of the tournament also offers several unique marketing and branding opportunities for your organization. Many of the golfers attending, particularly those coming as guests of your main sponsors and committee members, likely know very little about your particular organization. The following are suggested ways by which you can easily make these golfers more aware of your particular cause:

- set up an audio-visual display that explains what your organization does, who it benefits and how. This type of display can be presented at the tournament dinner or during the lunch or reception.

- If there is a particular brand, logo or slogan associated with your charity (e.g. a coloured ribbon) give each golfer a complimentary ribbon as they register and ask them to wear it throughout the day. Explain to them the significance of the ribbon as it relates to your organization.

- While on-course you can create awareness of your organization by providing statistics or facts about your particular cause in a fun and informative way (e.g. trivia contest at one hole)

- Include a short message in the program from your organization's executive director or senior volunteer, thanking the attendees and advising them how the proceeds will be used.

- A very effective method of "telling your story" is to have a volunteer speak briefly at the dinner as to how your organization has been of benefit to them.

In terms of branding opportunities, we recommend that a consistent brand or logo be used to associate the golf event with your charity. That brand may well be your existing organization's name or logo or you may want to create a golf-specific logo/brand/tournament name that reflects your organization's objectives. This brand/logo should be used consistently on all printed materials that are shown or distributed at the tournament, such as the rule sheet, dinner program, table cards, etc.

Post-Event Marketing

In your event follow up and thank you correspondence, there are additional opportunities to promote your organization and enhance your brand awareness. We recommend that:

- A thank you letter sent relatively soon after the tournament can not only thank all sponsors, golfers and donors but also inform these participants that your organization has raised X net dollars in support of the organization. Ideally, you should be as specific as possible in letting these supporters know how these proceeds will be used.

- Personally visit your key sponsors to not only present their organization with a certificate of thanks, but also individually acknowledge the contact person in that organization who arranged the sponsorship.

- Any opportunities to promote your event in the local media (e.g. picture of the cheque presentation at the dinner) will help build awareness of your organization.

- Email your golfers and sponsors and invite them to visit your website to download pictures from the tournament
- Send out an electronic pre-Christmas holiday greeting with a "Save the Date" message about next year's tournament.

 *Pro's Tip*

Some tournaments employ a variety of sales incentives to increase participation such as:

- ✓ *Early bird registration discount: 10% reduction if the registration fee is paid 90 days in advance of the tournament.*

- ✓ *Discount rate for a foursome (e.g. $125/player or $450/foursome.)*

- ✓ *Discount rate for the purchase of a hole sponsorship and foursome.*

- ✓ *Collect all golfers' names, addresses and email addresses at the tournament so you can build an even better database for next year's event. In compiling such a list, be sure that your organization is complying with all relevant privacy legislation.*

A SUCCESSFUL FUNDRAISING GOLF TOURNAMENT

SECTION K

Sponsorship Support – The Key to a Profitable Event

SECTION K

Sponsorship Support – The Key to a Profitable Event

The key to generating significant profit at a charity golf tournament is the type and amount of sponsorship support that is obtained. Most tournaments will generate 70-80% of their profit from sponsorship revenue. When approaching sponsors, your organization should take some time to think strategically about which companies to approach and how to approach them (e.g. in writing, in person, through a committee member). Some suggested strategies include:

- Determine who you want to approach to be your sponsors and select three target companies for each major sponsor category;

- Determine who needs to be approached in that company to approve your request

- Create a sponsorship package telling the prospective sponsor about your organization (include some facts and figures and who you are and what you do)

- Include a specific request – e.g. "would ABC Manufacturing be willing to invest $5000 in our organization to become the Dinner Sponsor for our upcoming charity golf tournament?"

- Outline the specific benefits the sponsor will receive in return for their support.

To attract sponsors the following strategies will work well:

Establish the Sponsorship Categories, Prices and Benefits

- How many sponsorship opportunities are there and at what price levels?
- What specific, tangible benefits does each sponsor receive for their contribution?
- How will these sponsors be recognized, thanked and cultivated for ongoing support?

Suggested Sponsor Categories

Title/Presenting Sponsor

- Major sponsor of the tournament
- Receives top billing/recognition in all promotional materials and mediums
- Usually receives at least one complimentary foursome in the tournament

Category Sponsor

- There are various "categories" that can be sponsored such as Lunch Sponsor, Dinner Sponsor, Cart Sponsor, Contest Sponsor, etc.
- Receives recognition linked to the specific category sponsored (e.g. cart sponsor has name/logo on each golf cart)

- Depending on the sponsorship level, these sponsors may also receive a complimentary foursome as one of their sponsor benefits

Hole/Tee Sponsors

- Generally the lowest cost sponsor level seeking the highest number of supporters
- Suggest limiting hole sponsors to a maximum of 2 sponsors per hole, so as not to dilute the value of the sponsorship

In Kind Sponsors

- Suppliers (e.g. printer) who provide a product or service at no charge (while this sponsorship does not generate revenue, it can significantly reduce tournament expenses).

Sponsor Recognition

Recognize your sponsors as much as possible leading up to the event, at the tournament and following the tournament. Suggested means of recognizing and thanking these sponsors are:

- List "sponsors to date" in the pre-tournament literature
- Post a "sponsors confirmed to date" list on the website and keep updating regularly
- Press release to announce sponsors
- Always acknowledge the sponsors in proportion to the financial value of their sponsorship.

At the Event

- Let sponsors put up signage in proportion to their level of support.

- Mention sponsors on collateral materials used at the tournament (e. rule sheet, event program)

- Allow sponsors to display their products or give out marketing information on their company.

- Mention and thank sponsors by name (and where appropriate mention the key individual representative from that company).

Post Event

- Mention the key sponsors in all follow up correspondence and thank you letters

- Start the sponsorship request process early as every sponsor company receives more requests than they can fulfill.

Pro's Tips

✓ *Sponsorships are often perceived as "expensive" and only available to large corporations. Why not include a more moderately priced sponsor level (e.g. tee sponsor at $250/tee) that may be attractive to smaller and medium-sized businesses?*

- ✓ *Offer a combined "hole sponsor/foursome package" with a small discount to encourage both sponsorship support and golfer registration*

- ✓ *Avoid conflicts at the category sponsor and title/event sponsor level (e.g. two banks getting equal billing)*

- ✓ *Offering three to four different priced sponsorship levels can work, but try to avoid offering so many different sponsorship levels that the sponsor prospect gets confused and loses interest.*

- ✓ *Make sure the golf course is aware of who your key sponsors are to avoid any conflicts with a key competitor who might be a supplier to that golf course (e.g. Coke as a key sponsor at a golf course that only carries Pepsi product).*

SECTION L
Golfer Gifts & Prizes

SECTION L

Golfer Gifts & Prizes

A key ingredient of any successful golf tournament is the quality of the prize table and the gift(s) each golfer brings home. In organizing this event the Committee should consider:

- What quantity of prizes are required and for what purposes? (to recognize the top golfers - team and individual and how many?)

- Will prizes be needed for raffle/auction purposes? Certain prizes may generate more revenue in a raffle (e.g. trip for two to Hawaii) than in a live/silent auction.

- Will every golfer receive a prize/gift? - and if so, is it a different prize per golfer? Getting 144 prizes for a full shotgun event can be very time-consuming. Instead, you may want to consider giving each golfer a "welcome gift" or "registration gift" package that is the same for all participants, and then focus on a smaller number of higher quality prizes for top golfers, the raffle, and the auction. If you choose to give each golfer a gift, this decision should be reflected in your budget and/or listed as a sponsorship opportunity.

Obtaining Prizes

Similar to the marketing efforts to attract golfers to the tournament, the Committee should compile a list of local businesses, suppliers to the organization benefiting from the proceeds, customers/suppliers of Committee members, etc. who can be approached for prizes. Some firms will donate a sample of their product while other firms, such as an insurance company, might provide tickets to sporting events, golf shirts, etc. for the prize table. Any donated item can generally be put to good use but the following is a list of items that are very popular golf tournament prizes:

- electronic items (TV, CD player, DVD player, phones, cell phones, palm pilots)
- gift certificates for restaurants, golf courses, hotels, spas
- sporting goods
- BBQs
- gift baskets – especially "themed" baskets of liquor products, food products, coffee/tea
- framed prints
- children's toys/games
- computer games/computer software
- sports memorabilia
- golf shirts, golf bags, golf balls, putters, rain suits, hats
- tools & appliances

Golfer Gifts

You should determine whether or not you want every golfer to receive a prize or gift and if so, is it a different prize per golfer. Obtaining 144 different prizes for a full shotgun event can be very time-consuming. Instead, you may want to consider giving each golfer a "welcome gift" or "registration gift" package that is the same for all participants and then focus on a smaller number of higher quality prizes for top golfers, the raffle, and the auction. If you choose to give each golfer a gift, this decision should be reflected in your budget and/or listed as a sponsorship opportunity. You should also give consideration to what kind of gift would best suit your golfers, meet your budget and reflect well on your organization. How the gift is distributed is also a key factor in enhancing the golfer's experience at your tournament. For example, if the gift is a large item such as, a travel bag, you may want to give it to each golfer as they drive in to the golf course and drop off their golf clubs so they do not have to walk back to their cars carrying a large item.

Pro's Tip

- ✓ Most companies require a written request even if the contact person is well known to the Committee. Create a standard "prize request" letter that each member of your committee can customize.

- ✓ Follow up the letter with a phone call no more than two weeks later.

- ✓ Ask the prospective donor for a set of foursome prizes, particularly if every golfer is to receive a prize.

- ✓ Prize donor recognition should be similar to sponsor recognition but not quite as prominent.

- ✓ Thank the prize donors at the event and in follow up letters.

- ✓ Be creative in getting prizes (e.g. golf lesson from the club pro, behind-the-scenes tour of a local television station, helicopter ride over a local attraction)

A SUCCESSFUL FUNDRAISING GOLF TOURNAMENT

SECTION M

Fundraising Activities at the Tournament

SECTION M

Fundraising Activities at the Tournament

The four main fundraising components in any charity golf tournament are:

- Player Registration Fees (see Section E)
- Sponsorship Support (see Section K)
- On-Course Activities (see Section H)
- Raffle/Auction (see Section M)

As noted earlier in this manual, it is imperative for the Committee to bear in mind how much money it is asking the golfer to contribute, either by way of registration fee and/or on-course activities. You should avoid "nickel and diming" your golfers by constantly asking them for money throughout the day, especially out on-course. This section will focus primarily on the raffle/auction component of revenue generation.

Raffle

Holding a raffle or draw at the tournament is a relatively easy way to generate additional revenue for your organization. One advantage to a raffle at the post-golf lunch or dinner is that the odds of winning (e.g., 1 in 150 people) are quite high. One option is to set aside a number of high quality prizes and sell raffle tickets for draws for these prizes. It is a good idea to let golfers know specifics about the raffle prizes perhaps by publishing a list of the prizes and their descriptions or by setting aside a "raffle prize table" that all golfers can visit during the post golf reception. Certain municipalities and jurisdictions may require that your organization obtain a raffle license if the prizes to be given out exceed a certain monetary amount. Please consult your local municipal clerk's office if there are any questions about legalities surrounding your raffle.

Auction

Auctions have become very commonplace at charity golf tournaments and can be a great source of revenue. However, a successful and profitable auction requires a significant amount of planning and effort to secure the right mix of items, prepare the bid sheets and auction displays and execute the auction itself. Your organization should consider one or both forms of auction:

Silent Auction

- Set up a number of quality items on the auction tables along with a bid sheet and description of the auction item. Your auction bid sheet should describe the item accurately, its retail value, the minimum bid accepted and the minimum increment by which bids will be increased. The donor of the auction item should also be clearly recognized on the auction bid sheet.

- Silent auctions generally attract good traffic as golfers want to see the items that are available. You can generate interest in these auction items by publishing a list of certain key auction items in advance and publicize these details to your golfers.

- Position the auction tables in a visible area to facilitate bidding, such as near the bar area or main entranceway to the dining room. Make sure there is enough space for the golfers to easily move through the auction area and make their bids.

- Keep the auction open to a certain time and then let everyone know when the auction will be closing. The emcee can advise the audience of the time left to bid.

- At a golf tournament we would recommend that the ideal number of items in a silent auction be based on the number of attendees at the dinner. As a guideline, we use a 15-20% ratio (e.g. aim for 21-28 items for a 144-person tournament).

- Carefully consider the kinds of items to include in your silent auction. We would recommend offering a variety of items that will appeal to a wide range of tastes and personal budgets, such as:

  Electronic items

  Gift certificates for restaurants, golf courses, hotels, spas

  Gift baskets – especially "themed" baskets of liquor products, food products, coffee/tea

  Items for children

  Computer games/computer software

> *Sports memorabilia – autographed items from well-recognized athletes are best, but do not overfill your auction with too many sports memorabilia items*
>
> *Tools & appliances*
>
> *Unique items or experiences are well received (backstage concert tickets, dinner for eight in your home catered by a local chef, foursome of golf at an exclusive private club)*
>
> *Packaging several smaller items is also profitable – limo ride, theatre tickets and an overnight stay in a local hotel*

Live Auction

Live auctions can also be a very good revenue generator but they are riskier than a silent auction in that the items tend to be larger in value and not all attendees will be willing to publicly bid on such items. To succeed at a live auction at a golf event you need:

- An auctioneer/emcee who is comfortable asking people to bid.

- Good items of high perceived value – limit the number of items from three to five.

- Willing audience members to participate in the bidding.

As with the silent auction, it is helpful to promote these items in advance to your attendees, particularly larger cost items such as golf trips, large screen televisions, etc. that may require the bidder to give more thought as to what he/she is willing to spend.

 Pro's Tips

✓ Set up a payment area beside the auction table so that the successful bidders can pay for their items easily and quickly.

✓ It will greatly facilitate the auction cash-out to set up several "pay stations" and to be able to accept credit card payments.

✓ Carefully consider whether a particular item will generate more revenue if it is in a silent auction or live auction

SECTION N

Immediately Prior to the Tournament

SECTION N

Immediately Prior to the Tournament

In the 30 days leading up to the tournament, there are a number of key tasks to focus on:

- Confirm the names and foursome groupings of each golfer.

- Send an electronic reminder notice to each golfer with the course map, tournament itinerary, any specific reminders (e.g. change in the starting time, confirmation of dietary requests)

- Send reminder notices to volunteers with details on-course location and map, what to wear, when to arrive, their specific duties at the event, etc.

- Design and print the event program, rules sheet, tickets or instructions for on-course contests (e.g. mulligans) and any other day-of-event materials.

- Provide the golf course with final golfer numbers/golfer names and food & beverage requirements.

- Finalize all sponsor signage, logos and corporate names and produce the signage

- Final pick up/delivery of prizes and gifts

- Prepare draft notes for the emcee and any other speakers/presenters.

- Prepare a detailed itinerary for the "day of the event" for review by your golf committee. This checklist/script should also indicate who is responsible for which activity/task and at which time.

- Prepare cash floats for on-course activities/raffle/auction.

- Prepare a list of key contact numbers that you may need for the day of the event, such as cell phone numbers for your golf committee members, key volunteers, golf course contacts, emcee, speakers/presenters/entertainers. This list should also contain contact information for anyone who is delivering a large prize or other significant delivery on the day of the event.

- Prepare a "tool box" or "event kit" for the day of the tournament. This box should include items such as pens, calculators, tape, scissors, first aid kit, highlighters, elastic bands, staplers, cash boxes, envelopes.

Pro's Tips

✓ For existing tournaments, review your notes from last year's tournament to determine if there were any crucial last minute issues that you can more proactively manage for this year's event.

✓ For new events, arrange to visit the golf course hosting your event on the day of another tournament to observe the flow of the tournament set up and the registration process.

A SUCCESSFUL FUNDRAISING GOLF TOURNAMENT

SECTION O
VOLUNTEER MANAGEMENT

SECTION O

Volunteer Management

A very important component of any successful charity golf tournament is the effective use of volunteer resources on the day of the tournament. Your organization should consider the following issues in determining how best to manage the volunteers:

How Many Volunteers Are Required

The number of volunteers will depend on several factors such as the size of your tournament, the number of on-course activities that need "staffing" and the number of non-golfing staff and committee members that are available to help at the tournament.

Create a matrix or chart of the various stations throughout the day that will require volunteers to man these activities. It is important to plan for people to help with:

- Pre-registration set up at the golf course (e.g. unloading vehicles, setting up golfer gift bags)

- Registration (checking golfers in, selling any passports/activities, distributing gifts, etc)

- On-course – manning the on-course contests

- Post-golf reception – assisting with areas such as dinner seating, raffle sales, silent auction

- Event wrap up – auction cash out, collecting left-over prizes and gifts, loading vehicles with signage and other items to be returned to your organization

What Volunteers Need to Know

It is important that your volunteers be well prepared prior to the event so you do not have to spend a lot of time preparing them on the day of the actual tournament. You should convey the following information to the volunteers:

- Directions to the golf course
- Their arrival time and departure time
- What to wear – ideally running shoes, shorts, golf shirt, hat and jacket
- An on site contact person to check in with when they arrive
- Whether or not meals will be provided for them
- Some basic information about your organization, the tournament itself and the types of roles they will be carrying out

In turn, it is important that you obtain the following information from your volunteers, particularly if you do not personally know them in advance of the event:

- Their cell phone number and full name
- What hours they are available to help out/do they have to leave early

- Any restrictions on their ability to assist at the tournament (e.g. medical condition, aversion to the sun, etc).

Managing Volunteers at the Tournament

In order to most effectively use these volunteers at the tournament, you should:

- Assign one key staff member or committee member to be the volunteer coordinator

- Where possible assign the volunteers to work in pairs (although this may not always be feasible)

- Have a brief meeting with your volunteers the morning of the event to give them their assignments and answer any questions

- As much as possible, give the volunteers instructions in writing (secured on a clipboard) so the instructions are clearly outlined and can be easily passed on to a new volunteer taking the next shift at that station

- Make sure the volunteers can contact you or your volunteer coordinator throughout the day by cellphone or two-way radio.

- Try and visually identify your volunteers by name-tag, t-shirt or hat with the organization's name and logo (another branding opportunity)

- Be cognizant of the weather, especially heat and try to rotate your volunteers so that no-one is left out on-course for five to six hours without a break

- Give the golf course a list of which volunteers will be at which holes so the course can provide chairs at that hole, a table if necessary and ideally a golf cart for the volunteers.
- Make sure the on-course marshals (rangers who patrol the course) know where your volunteers are located, in case of an emergency (such as a lightning storm).

How and Where To Recruit Your Volunteers

There are several sources you can use to recruit your volunteers:

- Existing staff or volunteers within or associated with your organization
- Non-golfing Board members (current & former), committee members and supporters of your organization
- Ask your sponsors if they want to involve any of their personnel
- Students looking to fulfill local community service hours

    Contact your local high school, college or university; (keep in mind that certain volunteer roles, such as witnessing a Hole-In-One contest, will have age restrictions)

- Many corporations have programs by which their employees are encouraged to support a local charity event as a volunteer. Contact your local Chamber of Commerce or business association for more details.

Post-Event Follow up With Volunteers

After the event you should:

- Thank your volunteers in writing (you'll need them again next year!)

- Ask for their input on the tournament – being on the front lines all day, they might be hearing feedback/comments from the golfers that will be helpful in evaluating and improving the tournament

 Pro's Tips

✓ Feed and water the volunteers, especially those out on-course – it keeps them happy and healthy

✓ Thank your volunteers both on the day of the tournament, in the program and ideally with a thank you letter and/or small token of appreciation afterwards.

SECTION P
On the First Tee - Day-of-Event Management

SECTION P

On the First Tee - Day-of-Event Management

It's now the day of the event. The following is a checklist of items that your organization should follow to make sure the tournament runs smoothly:

- Get set up at the course early and establish a "headquarters" area near the registration table/greeting station.

- Check in with the course contact and review last minute changes (e.g. player name updates in specific foursomes.)

- Certain items (e.g. signage) need to go out on the course early in the day. Pre-arrange the delivery of these items with the golf course .

- Bring a "tool box" of supplies - cash box, float, pens, markers, tape, calculator, cell phone, credit card processing machine and receipts, etc.

- Check in with your office (or your own voicemail/email) for last minute player changes.

- Have a volunteer check the golfer names on each cart - the course needs to be told about name changes/spelling errors.

- Assign a volunteer to staff the registration desk early as there are always a few keen golfers who arrive much earlier than expected.

- Get any necessary tickets/tokens/etc. from the pro shop staff for distribution at registration.
- Check on any food and beverage requirements - will it be ready at the designated time? Are there tickets to give to each golfer for them to redeem at the lunch?
- Golf club rentals - if any player has requested them, doublecheck that the course has them ready.
- Distribute any items that need to be placed on the golf carts.

Volunteers

- Have all non-golfing volunteers meet at the registration area and give them a brief orientation of the day's itinerary and the course layout. They will be asked where the locker rooms are, when lunch is, etc.!
- Give the volunteers their assignments and name tags and advise any one going out to a hole when the tournament starts to eat lunch early/bring a snack etc.
- If possible, assign one person to look after the volunteers out on the course, and ensure they rotate their assignments and are not "stranded" at a hole. Make sure that volunteers have food/drink throughout the day as well as protection/shade from the heat and sun. A chair and an umbrella for volunteers at a designated hole is a good idea.

Registration

- There will undoubtedly be last minute player changes, so assign one person to handle registration and another to coordinate cart/name changes with the golf course.

- A good sequence for player registration is:

    Greet the golfers and thank them for coming

    Give them their starting hole and/or tee time

    Remind them about lunch/driving range/etc.

    Give them their tickets/tokens as applicable

    Sell them the golf contest package (ensure those selling have floats, cash box, etc)

    Give them their gift

    Thank them again for coming

- Greeting and thanking the golfers is a terrific opportunity for a senior staff member or volunteer from your organization to personally interact with each golfer. Carefully consider who to place at this station and where to locate this person relative to your registration area.

- Some golfers will drop off their last minute prize donations at registration, so be ready to receive these items and note what item was brought in and by whom.

Getting The Golfers Out on The Course

- Depending on the starting format and number of golfers, you will need to work closely with the golf course staff to get the tournament started on time.

- Most courses will have a P.A. system or loudspeaker to ask golfers to go to their carts or call foursomes by tee time to the first tee.

- At registration tell your golfers to be in their carts at a certain time – we recommend 10 minutes before the actual start of the shotgun.

While the Golf Tournament is Underway

- Give the registration table volunteers a chance to regroup and update their registration lists.

- Keep the registration table open about 30 minutes after the scheduled starting time to allow for any latecomers.

- Setup:

    prize table

    auction

    display on the charity

- Relocate banners and signage as necessary.

- Confirm all dinner arrangements with catering staff.

- Distribute dinner program and any other items required to each place setting.

- Test the microphone and any AV equipment required.
- Go out and check on the tournament - is the pace of play as it should be? How are the golfers enjoying themselves?

Post-golf Reception/dinner

- Collect scorecards in coordination with pro shop staff.
- Complete scoring and prepare winners' names on an easy-to-read list that the emcee can use later.
- During dinner move the silent auction items into the dining room to facilitate bidding.
- Go table to table handing out any additional prizes/tickets/gifts to the golfers (e.g. foursome photographs.)

Before Dinner

The emcee should:

- Welcome everyone prior to dinner and then thank all for coming.
- Remind everyone of the evening's itinerary.

After Dinner

The emcee should:

- Call up a representative of the charity who in turn should thank the sponsors and explain how the proceeds will be used.
- Introduce the guest speaker/entertainment as applicable.

- Close off the auction at the designated time.
- Hold the raffle.
- Involve committee members here as a way to publicly thank and recognize their efforts.
- Announce and distribute the prizes.

Note: This order can be varied but it is usually better to distribute the prizes last as a way to keep the interest of the audience.

Wrap Up/breakdown

- Committee members should collect any unclaimed prizes/gifts
- Collect sponsor signage and banners
- Determine how cash receipts will be handled and/or deposited and by whom

 ## Pro's Tips

✓ Ensure that the same team of at least two people should be in control of cash at all times, from start to finish until it is placed in a safe, or turned over to a bank or some official body which can take responsibility for it. For obvious reasons of personal safety and public accountability, individuals - no matter how high a level of responsibility they may have - should never allow themselves to be left alone with public monies.

✓ For the tournament create two sets of player lists - one that shows the foursomes by starting hole or tee time in consecutive order, and a second list by alphabetical order based on the player's last name. These lists should be made available to all volunteers, as well as the golf course staff, as they will be very handy throughout the day.

SECTION Q

Birdies & Bogeys - Contingency Planning/ Pitfalls to Avoid

SECTION Q

Birdies & Bogeys - Contingency Planning/ Pitfalls to Avoid

Murphy's Law (whatever can go wrong, will go wrong) can also apply to a golf tournament, no matter how well planned. Therefore, your organization should prepare some contingency plans for the following events.

Inclement Weather

The biggest variable for any golf tournament is the weather. In your initial discussions with the golf course get a clear indication of their specific "rain policy" including alternative date options, fixed costs charged to the tournament, etc. The course will want the tournament to proceed unless the course is unplayable due to severe rain, thunder or lightning. In the event of a complete rainout and cancellation, send volunteers to the course to greet golfers who may have already arrived at the golf course.

In the event of a rain delay on the course, bear in mind that golfers by and large will not be put off by a short rain delay or brief shower. If the weather is bad enough to bring golfers in, consult with the course pro about revised scoring (e.g. base it on 9 holes) or make all prizes random draws. You can also set up some indoor contests (e.g. putting, golf videos) in cooperation with the clubhouse staff. The key to managing bad weather is constant communication – both with the golf course and with your golfers.

Rental Clubs

Invariably some golfer shows up without clubs and needs to rent them. In your planning ask the course what quantity of rental clubs they have available, what is the cost, etc. You will also need to advise the golf course if rental clubs are to be paid by the individual requesting them or put on the "master invoice" for the tournament.

Shortfall in Donated Prizes

Sometimes a golf committee realizes two weeks before the event that there are fewer prizes donated than anticipated. In this instance you may need to spend money on prizes. If so, approach a local retailer (golf or otherwise) about providing prizes at cost in return for recognition at the tournament.

Pitfalls to Avoid

There are some specific "pitfalls to avoid" in organizing a golf tournament. We recommend:

- If you are the key organizer, try to not tie yourself down with specific tasks like selling raffle tickets or registering golfers. Rather, you should be operating more as a "supervisor/manager", able to oversee the entire event and respond proactively to any issues that may arise.

- Resist the temptation to oversell the tournament. 144 golfers is the capacity for most courses for an 18 hole shotgun start event (two foursomes starting on each hole, back to back). Going to 152 or 160 golfers will significantly slow down the pace of play.

- Keep it interesting - there are many golf tournaments raising money for worthwhile causes, so the competition to attract golfers to your event is quite high. Try to establish your event as a well-organized, enjoyable, fun tournament.

- "Our Celebrity Guest Left After Nine Holes" – if you involve a local celebrity make sure they or their representatives fully understand what is expected of them at the tournament. One suggestion is to send them a written outline of the tournament, including what time they should arrive, their specific role (e.g. play with the title sponsor, hand out the winning foursome prizes, etc) and a contact name and number at the tournament.

- Refer to the golf course's dress code in your marketing material. Most courses have a dress code (e.g. no jeans, no collarless shirts), and you can avoid having a golfer inadvertently embarrassed by telling your golfers in advance what the dress code requirements are.

- Set realistic expectations - especially in the first year of the tournament, carefully consider what expectations there are regarding number of golfers, number of sponsors, net profit and tie these expectations into the objectives the Committee sets out for the tournament.

A SUCCESSFUL FUNDRAISING GOLF TOURNAMENT

SECTION R

The Scorecard - Tournament Review and Follow up

SECTION R

The Scorecard - Tournament Review and Follow up

After the tournament has finished there are several "follow up" initiatives that the Committee should undertake:

a) Financial Report - prepare a statement on the tournament's revenues, expenses and profit. If there are any outstanding receivables or invoices, these should be addressed as soon as possible.

b) Create a database of golfers, donors, sponsors and suppliers both for thank you letter/tax receipt purposes and for mailing out for next year's event.

c) Get some customer feedback - this can come from Committee members talking to their friends and colleagues. Then measure the results to see which objectives were met and how, and which were not and why not.

d) Debrief the tournament with the golf course staff and get their input on what went right, what went wrong and where to improve for next year. A tentative date for next year's event should also be booked at this time.

e) The Committee should meet to review the tournament and make a list of recommendations for next year's event.

f) Files, reports, and documentation from the Committee should be organized and put in storage so it can be easily accessed next year.

SECTION 5

Good to Great – Taking your Tournament to the Next Level

SECTION S

Good to Great – Taking your Tournament to the Next Level

Once you have established your tournament as a profitable, well- organized event, it is easy to become complacent. There are several strategies your organization can employ to not only increase the net profit but also continue to build your event (and create greater brand awareness for your organization) by continually striving to turn a good event into a great charity golf tournament.

The Venue

You should consider the host course a key partner in this event. Seek their input on what you can do to take your tournament to the next level and, in the course of these discussions, get the course to more actively support your tournament. If you sense that your golfers might want to change courses after several years, embark on a site search as outlined in Section D. It is a good idea to survey golfers before changing courses to get their input on alternative locations, price point sensitivity and geographical restrictions.

The Cause

Celebrate the success of your previous golf events and use milestones (e.g. 10th Anniversary of the tournament, reaching

$250,000 in net profit) to recognize and thank your supporters. Many tournaments will annually acknowledge their "5 year" and "10 year" participants.

The Extras

Well-run golf tournaments tend to have a high rate of retention, so many of the same golfers will return each year. Keep their interest by adding in new twists to the event, perhaps one or two each year.

Examples include:

- Varied entertainment at the dinner each year
- Golf club demonstration on the driving range by a leading supplier
- Introduce a warm-up stretching clinic or back massage service
- Create a theme each year
- Complimentary club cleaning
- Video swing analysis
- Different variations to the scoring format
- New on-course contests
- Combine the "golf" event with another activity "FINS & SKINS" (golf & fishing), golf & gambling, etc.

The Survey

One of the best methods of continually improving your tournament is to ask your attendees for their input. You can ask them to fill out a simple one-page, five-question survey at the dinner or email that survey out right after the tournament. Get their feedback on key areas such as choice of golf course, tournament format, pace of play, prizes, gifts, food and beverage and overall organization, and then use their suggestions to improve the next tournament.

SECTION T
How GTI Can Further Assist Your Organization

SECTION T

How GTI Can Further Assist Your Organization

As the previous sections demonstrate, there is a great deal of pre-planning, attention to detail, managing numerous tasks simultaneously and effective implementation that all needs to be carried out to produce a successful charitable golf tournament.

Golf Tournaments Incorporated can assist your organization with all aspects of tournament planning and day-of-event coordination as described in this handbook. GTI offers both a "consulting fee" service for tournament assistance in certain key areas, as well as a more extensive "full service event management" package.

Please contact Frank MacGrath, President of GTI for further details and cost estimates.

Office: 905-726-4488
Email: fmacgrath@gtigolf.com
website: www.gtigolf.com

Golf Tournament Planning Resources

The following is a list of organizations and associations that may be of benefit to you in planning your next golf tournament:

Golf Association of Ontario
www.goa.ca

Royal Canadian Golf Association
www.rcga.org

PGA of America
www.pga.com

National Golf Course Owners Association
www.ngcoa.ca

Hole-In-One Canada
www.Hole-In-One.ca

Golf's Yellow Pages
www.golfsyellowpages.com

Were we up to par?

If you've found this Handbook helpful in planning and executing your golf fundraiser,

We have more copies for your event team at a huge Previous Client Discount.

Fill out the Order Form below, tear out the entire page, and send it to us with payment. Use the rates shown, skip the GST, and call us for orders of more than ten copies for an even deeper discount.

We'll have your event management team playing at par in no time!

2-5 COPIES -- $25.90 EACH;   6-10 COPIES -- $22.20 EACH

No of Copies Needed _____   Total Cost $ _____

❏ Cheque/Money Order enclosed   ❏ VISA   ❏ MasterCard

Number _____
Expiry _____ / _____

Name _____
Title _____
Organization _____
Address _____
City/Town _____
Postal Code _____
Tel Fax _____
E-Mail _____

SEND WITH PAYMENT TO:
CIVIL SECTOR PRESS, BOX 86, STATION C, TORONTO, ON M6J 3M7
TEL: 416-345-9403   FAX: 416-345-8010   EMAIL: INFO@HILBORN.COM

Frank MacGrath

Frank MacGrath is the President of Golf Tournaments Incorporated, a Toronto-based golf-event management company. Founded in 1993, Golf Tournaments Incorporated (GTI) has planned, organized and implemented hundreds of successful fundraising golf tournaments at golf courses throughout Canada, as well as numerous specialty golf events, hole in one contests and other golf-related activities. GTI has worked with a wide variety of charities, corporations and not for profit organizations across Canada including the Bloorview Kids Rehab Foundation, Child Find Ontario, Parkinson Society Canada, Rose Cherry's Home for Kids, Lymphoma Foundation Canada, Youth in Motion, Canadian Venture Capital Association and the Bay Street Children's Foundation.

Prior to purchasing Golf Tournaments Incorporated, Frank was a senior executive with the Miller Group of Companies (Miller Paving, McAsphalt Industries and related companies) from 1987-1997. While at Miller as Vice-President of Real Estate, Frank coordinated the rezoning, rehabilitation and development of several of Miller's industrial lands into industrial projects, golf properties, and housing developments.

Frank has a Masters Degree in Public Administration from Queen's University, as well as a Bachelor of Arts degree from the University of Toronto. Frank has been an active community member, holding volunteer leadership positions including: President, University of Toronto Alumni Association, UTM Alumni House Cabinet Co-Chair, and Board Member, Parkinson Society Canada.

www.ingramcontent.com/pod-product-compliance
Lightning Source LLC
Chambersburg PA
CBHW051525230426
43668CB00012B/1748